Glendale Library, Arts & Culture Dept.

3 9 0 1 0 0 5 5 7 2 6 5 3 7

MONTROSE

D0788639

SPOTLIGHT ON NATIVE AMERICANS

WAMPANOAG

Joseph Stanley

PowerKiDS
press.

New York

j 970.3 Wampanoag STA

Published in 2016 by The Rosen Publishing Group, Inc.
29 East 21st Street, New York, NY 10010

Copyright © 2016 by The Rosen Publishing Group, Inc.

All rights reserved. No part of this book may be reproduced in any form without permission in writing from the publisher, except by a reviewer.

First Edition

Editor: Katie Kawa
Book Design: Samantha DeMartin
Material reviewed by: Donald A. Grinde, Jr., Professor of Transnational/American Studies at the State University of New York at Buffalo.

Photo Credits: Cover, pp. 5, 15, 21, 23, 27, 29 Boston Globe/Boston Globe/Getty Images; pp. 6–7 Loop Images/Universal Images Group/Getty Images; p. 9 John Kropewnicki/Shutterstock.com; p. 11 Universal History Archive/Universal Images Group/Getty Images; pp. 13, 17 MPI/Archive Photos/Getty Images; p. 14 Jannis Tobias Werner/Shutterstock.com; p. 16 courtesy of the Library of Congress; pp. 18–19 dp Photography/Shutterstock.com; p. 25 Slowking4/Wikimedia Commons; p. 26 Frederick M. Brown/Getty Images Entertainment/Getty Images.

Library of Congress Cataloging-in-Publication Data

Stanley, Joseph, author.
  Wampanoag / Joseph Stanley.
     pages cm. — (Spotlight on Native Americans)
  Includes index.
  ISBN 978-1-5081-4145-7 (pbk.)
  ISBN 978-1-5081-4146-4 (6 pack)
  ISBN 978-1-5081-4148-8 (library binding)
  1. Wampanoag Indians—Juvenile literature. I. Title.
  E99.W2S74 2016
  974.4004'97348—dc23
                              2015034691

Manufactured in the United States of America

CPSIA Compliance Information: Batch #BW16PK: For Further Information contact Rosen Publishing, New York, New York at 1-800-237-9932

CONTENTS

A LONG HISTORY
CHAPTER 1

The Wampanoag people are known for being the first Native Americans to interact with the Pilgrims upon their arrival in North America. However, the Wampanoag have a history that stretches back long before their first contact with European settlers. The Wampanoag and their **ancestors** have been living in what are now the states of Rhode Island and Massachusetts for thousands of years.

Like many Native American peoples, the Wampanoag population greatly decreased after Europeans came to North America. While there were once more than 40,000 Wampanoag, there are now only around 4,500 Wampanoag **descendants** living in the United States. Although their numbers may be much smaller than they once were, the Wampanoag are still working hard to preserve their traditional **culture**, especially their language.

There are two federally recognized Wampanoag groups in Massachusetts: the Mashpee Wampanoag Tribe and the Aquinnah Wampanoag Tribe, which is also known as the Wampanoag Tribe of Gay Head. Other communities of Wampanoag people have been recognized by the state of Massachusetts but not by the U.S. government.

Plimoth Plantation in Massachusetts, shown here, allows people to learn more about Wampanoag history and culture by putting them in the middle of a re-creation of a Wampanoag homesite from the time of the Pilgrims' arrival.

PEOPLE OF THE FIRST LIGHT

CHAPTER 2

The name "Wampanoag" means different things depending on who's translating it. It could mean "people of the dawn," "people of the first light," or "people of the east." Wampanoag peoples sometimes refer to themselves by one of these names.

These "people of the east" have their roots in the lands of eastern Rhode Island and southeastern Massachusetts. They still call these areas home today. Wampanoag homelands include the islands of Martha's Vineyard and Nantucket. The Wampanoag didn't believe in owning this land. They believed in sharing and working together to fish and farm.

According to traditional Wampanoag beliefs, the islands these people call home were formed by a giant named Moshup. Moshup was also responsible for turning the Aquinnah Cliffs on Martha's Vineyard red. He did this by throwing whales against the cliffs before he ate them.

The blood of the whales stained the cliffs, giving them their red coloring. Moshup plays a role in the creation stories told by many Native American groups along the northeastern coast of the United States, including the Mohegan people.

Moshup Beach is located right below the Aquinnah Cliffs on Martha's Vineyard. This beach was named for the giant who the Wampanoag people believe created the island.

FINDING FOOD

CHAPTER 3

The lands the Wampanoag call home have played a large part in every aspect of their lives—from their religious beliefs to their diet. Living near water helped the Wampanoag people become good fishers. They used wooden canoes they made themselves to fish. Hunting deer and gathering shellfish also provided the Wampanoag with food. Wampanoag peoples continue to hunt and fish for food today.

Corn, beans, and squash were three of the most important crops grown by Wampanoag women. The crops were often called "the three sisters" because they were planted together. The bean and squash vines grew around the corn stalks. The squash vines covered the ground to take in water and stop **erosion**. The beans added **nitrogen**, which all plants need to grow, to the soil.

Another important food in Wampanoag culture is the cranberry. Cranberry Day is a traditional harvesting celebration centered on the cranberry bogs that's still celebrated today. Cranberry Day is a day for Wampanoag elders to teach the next generation about their history and traditions.

Members of the Wampanoag community celebrate Cranberry Day every October. It's one of the most important celebrations in modern Wampanoag culture. Children are even allowed to take time off from school on this special day.

EARLY WAMPANOAG LEADERSHIP

CHAPTER 4

Early Wampanoag communities were led by respected men and women called *sachems*. Each community had its own *sachem*, but they were all united under one larger group, or confederacy. This larger group was governed by a person who held the title of *Massasoit*, which means "Great Leader."

A *sachem* was responsible for leading their community through planting and harvesting seasons. They also settled disagreements between people. They took care of the entire community, but they weren't alone in their leadership. A *sachem* was advised by councils made up of members of their community. Different councils represented different groups of people, such as Wampanoag women. A *sachem* who failed to show wisdom and leadership soon lost the respect and support of their people.

A *sachem* had another job that became even more important as the years went on: They represented their community when interacting with outsiders. When European settlers arrived in North America, *sachems* were the first Wampanoag people to formally meet with them.

Shown here is an illustration of a Wampanoag *sachem* meeting with European settlers.

MAKING PEACE WITH THE PILGRIMS

CHAPTER 5

The Wampanoag people had interactions with other groups of Europeans before they met the Pilgrims. Traders, explorers, and men hunting for gold were the first Europeans the Wampanoag met. These people sometimes **abducted** members of Wampanoag communities, and they brought diseases to North America that killed many Native Americans, including Wampanoag peoples.

However, in 1620, a new group of Europeans reached what later became known as Massachusetts. When the Pilgrims got off the *Mayflower*, they came onto Wampanoag lands. While the Wampanoag people stayed away from them at first, they eventually went to speak with these new settlers.

In 1621, the Pilgrims signed a peace **treaty** with the Wampanoag people. They mainly interacted with the community's *Massasoit*, who was named Ousamequin. However, the Pilgrims mistook his title for his name, so they referred to him as *Massasoit*. That same year, the Pilgrims wrote of a harvest celebration they shared with members of the Wampanoag community, which is often considered the first Thanksgiving.

The Pilgrims and the Wampanoag taught each other. The Wampanoag peoples learned about Christianity from the Pilgrims, and the Pilgrims learned how to live off the land from the Wampanoag people.

The peace treaty between the Wampanoag people and the Pilgrims lasted for more than 50 years.

A HARVARD EDUCATION

CHAPTER 6

One of the ways settlers tried to introduce Christianity to the Wampanoag people was through schools. Harvard University was established in 1636 as the first university in what later became the United States. However, it struggled financially at first. One way officials at Harvard believed they could get people in England to give them money for their school was to show they were **converting** Native Americans to Christianity.

With this idea in mind, Harvard Indian College opened around 1655. Its goal was to educate Native Americans with the hope that they would spread Christianity in their

Harvard University

Tiffany Smalley, shown here, graduated from Harvard in 2011. She was the first Wampanoag to graduate from this school since Caleb Cheeshahteaumuck did so in 1665.

communities. European settlers felt this would cause Native Americans to begin to move away from their traditional way of life, which would, in turn, make it easier to take over their lands.

Two of the first Native Americans to complete their studies at Harvard were members of the Wampanoag community named Joel Iacoomes and Caleb Cheeshahteaumuck. Iacoomes died not long before their graduation ceremony in 1665. In 2011, he was honored with a special degree from the school.

KING PHILIP'S WAR

CHAPTER 7

Although the relationship between the Wampanoag people and the Pilgrims started as one of peace, it didn't stay that way for long. As more settlers arrived from England, **tensions** began to rise.

In 1662, Ousamequin's son Metacomet (sometimes called Metacom) became *sachem*. To the English, he was known as King Philip. In 1675, the English killed three Wampanoag men whom they believed were responsible for killing another Wampanoag who'd converted to Christianity. This angered Metacomet, and it proved to be one of the final acts on the path to war.

Metacomet (King Philip)

King Philip's War lasted only around a year, but it was a bloody war. Wampanoag warriors **raided** English settlements, and English soldiers burned Wampanoag homes. In December 1675, the English attacked a **Narragansett** fort housing Wampanoag people in Rhode Island. Many Native Americans, including women and children, were killed in this attack, which came to be known as the Great Swamp Fight.

Metacomet was killed in August 1676. That marked the end of a war that led to the deaths of thousands of Native Americans and the near-destruction of the entire Wampanoag community.

King Philip's War, shown here, is known as one of the deadliest conflicts in the history of the United States.

FEDERAL RECOGNITION

CHAPTER 8

Despite their greatly reduced numbers, the Wampanoag worked to hold on to their traditional way of life. Once the 13 English colonies became the United States, the Wampanoag continued to keep their culture alive and to live in parts of their ancestral homelands. Other Native American communities were removed from their homelands and were forced to **migrate** to other parts of the country. However, communities of Wampanoag people remained in **New England**, and they still live there today.

In Massachusetts, the towns of Aquinnah and Mashpee have been strongholds of Wampanoag culture for centuries. In 1987, the federal government recognized the Aquinnah Wampanoag community. This group's land is located on the western end of Martha's Vineyard. In 2007, the Mashpee Wampanoag joined the Aquinnah Wampanoag as a federally recognized Native American group. The Mashpee Wampanoag lands are located on Cape Cod. By granting the Aquinnah Wampanoag Tribe and the Mashpee Wampanoag Tribe federal recognition, the U.S. government formally recognized and supported their ability to govern themselves.

In 1870, the town of Gay Head, Massachusetts, was built on traditional Wampanoag lands on Martha's Vineyard. When the Aquinnah Wampanoag Tribe was first recognized by the federal government, it was named the Wampanoag Tribe of Gay Head. However, in 1998, the town's name was changed to Aquinnah, and the tribe's name was changed to reflect that. The word "Aquinnah" means "end of the island" in the Wampanoag language.

COUNCILS AND COMMITTEES

CHAPTER 9

Each Wampanoag tribe has its own governing body, which is called a tribal council. The council is led by a chairperson, and underneath that position is the vice-chairperson. Each council also has a secretary and a treasurer, in addition to general council members.

Two council positions are held by traditional leaders. A chief is seen as the traditional leader of a specific Wampanoag group, and the chief has a permanent spot on the council. A medicine man is seen as a spiritual and physical healer in traditional Wampanoag culture. Each council has a medicine man, and medicine men also keep their spot on the council for life. Council meetings are open to all members of that specific Wampanoag group. This allows everyone to have a say in how their community is run. Wampanoag peoples also vote on issues that affect the whole community.

In addition to the tribal council, smaller committees exist for each tribe. Committees discuss important matters, such as public safety, health, and economic development.

Shown here is Beverly M. Wright, who served for a time as the chairperson of the Aquinnah Wampanoag Tribe.

MODERN WAMPANOAG LIFE

CHAPTER 10

Both the Mashpee Wampanoag Tribe and the Aquinnah Wampanoag Tribe continue their people's long tradition of working with the natural world around them. Both tribes operate shellfish farms to take advantage of the abundance of shellfish, such as oysters, around their lands. These tribes also run other businesses on their lands to provide jobs for their people.

Wampanoag people also work in cultural centers and other places that aim to preserve their traditional way of life and teach others about it. Some work at Plimoth Plantation, teaching visitors about past and present Wampanoag culture. Others work at the Aquinnah Cultural Center, which was created as a place for Aquinnah Wampanoag people to express their **heritage** in ways that allow visitors to learn about their community.

Each Wampanoag community also works to provide social services for its people. These services include affordable housing and access to good health care. Education is also important in Wampanoag communities. For example, the Mashpee Wampanoag Tribe has an education department designed to promote learning among young community members. This includes learning about Wampanoag history and the relationship between the Wampanoag people and the natural world.

Fishing has always been important to the Wampanoag way of life because Wampanoag communities are coastal communities.

RECLAIMING THEIR LANGUAGE

CHAPTER 11

Modern Wampanoag peoples are working to bring back parts of their culture that were lost for hundreds of years. One of the most important parts is their language. The Wampanoag language is part of the Algonquian language family. It was the first Native American language to use an alphabet for writing. Reading and writing were common skills among early Wampanoag peoples, but the language all but disappeared during the nineteenth century.

However, a project started in 1993 to restore this language as a common means of communication and expression among Wampanoag peoples. The Wampanoag Language **Reclamation** Project has brought together Wampanoag peoples from different groups who are united in their fight to bring back the language once used throughout their homelands.

The Wampanoag Language Reclamation Project began under the direction of Jessie "Little Doe" Baird, a

Mashpee Wampanoag woman who studied Algonquian **linguistics** at the Massachusetts Institute of Technology. She now teaches classes in the Wampanoag language for learners of all ages. She's also working with others to build a Wampanoag language dictionary.

Jessie "Little Doe" Baird

The Wampanoag language was dead for more than 150 years, but the hard work of Baird and her team has given it new life. This language was the first in the United States to be reclaimed after going through a period in which no native speakers were alive in the country.

SHARING WAMPANOAG STORIES

CHAPTER 12

Baird is just one of many Wampanoag people working hard to preserve the traditional Wampanoag way of life. Another famous member of the Wampanoag Language Reclamation Project is Joan Tavares Avant. Like Baird, Avant is a Mashpee Wampanoag woman who has devoted much of her life to the preservation of Wampanoag culture. Avant has served as a tribal historian, and her interest in Wampanoag history led her to publish a book in 2010 titled *People of the First Light*. This book was Avant's attempt to offer the Wampanoag view of their own history, as she found many accounts of their history were told by people outside of her community.

Another Wampanoag who's doing his part to teach others

Jonathan Perry

about his people's history is Jonathan Perry. Perry is an Aquinnah Wampanoag actor and artist who's appeared in television productions such as *Desperate Crossing: The Untold Story of the Mayflower*, which aired on The History Channel. Perry also works at Plimoth Plantation and travels to different places to speak about Wampanoag history and culture.

Jonathan Perry can be seen on the left in this photo taken at Plimoth Plantation in 2008. He's dressed in traditional Wampanoag clothing.

COMING TOGETHER TO CELEBRATE

CHAPTER 12

Each Wampanoag community has events throughout the year to honor their heritage. The Mashpee Wampanoag Tribe has held a powwow every year for more than 90 years. The powwow is held every July and lasts for three days. During this time, the Wampanoag people take part in spiritual ceremonies, traditional dance and drumming contests, and traditional arts, crafts, and cooking.

Members of the Aquinnah Wampanoag Tribe hold their own powwow every September. They also hold a Spring Social where they feast and celebrate the change of seasons from winter to spring. Cranberry Day is another day the Aquinnah Wampanoag set aside every year to celebrate as a community.

The Wampanoag people have had strong ties to their northeastern homelands for centuries. Although they're fewer in number than they once were, they're working together to reclaim their language and to share their culture with those who want to learn more about the community's rich history. Through the efforts of today's Wampanoag men and women, the community's traditional culture will live on for generations to come.

The proud members of Wampanoag communities who work at Plimoth Plantation, such as the man shown here, are doing their part to educate people about Wampanoag history and traditions in a personal and memorable way.

GLOSSARY

abduct: To take a person away by force.

ancestor: Someone in your family who lived long before you.

convert: To change from one thing into another.

culture: The beliefs and ways of life of a certain group of people.

descendant: Someone related to a person or group of people who lived at an earlier time.

erosion: The wearing away of the earth's surface by wind or water.

heritage: The traditions and beliefs that are part of the history of a group or nation.

linguistics: The scientific study of language.

migrate: To move from one place to another.

Narragansett: A group of Native Americans who lived in what's now Rhode Island and spoke a language in the Algonquian language family.

New England: The northeastern United States, which is made up of the states of Maine, New Hampshire, Vermont, Massachusetts, Rhode Island, and Connecticut.

nitrogen: A chemical with no taste or smell that makes up a large part of Earth's atmosphere and is present in all living things.

raid: To attack an enemy in a sudden and unexpected way.

reclamation: The process of getting back something that was lost or taken away.

tension: A state in which people or groups disagree with and feel anger toward each other.

treaty: An official agreement made between two or more countries or groups.

FOR MORE INFORMATION

BOOKS

Benoit, Peter, and Kevin Cunningham. *The Wampanoag.* New York, NY: Children's Press, 2011.

Mandell, Daniel R. *King Philip's War: The Conflict Over New England.* New York, NY: Chelsea House, 2007.

Riehecky, Janet. *The Wampanoag: The People of the First Light.* Mankato, MN: Bridgestone Books, 2003.

WEBSITES

Due to the changing nature of Internet links, PowerKids Press has developed an online list of websites related to the subject of this book. This site is updated regularly. Please use this link to access the list: www.powerkidslinks.com/sona/wamp

INDEX